# Pongalo Pongal!
The Tamil Festival of Harvest

Written By: Lakshmi Narayani

Illustrated By: Lakshmi Narayani and Suresh Krishnan

© 2020 Lakshmi Narayani

All rights reserved. Except as may be permitted by the Copyright Act, no part of this publication may be reproduced in any form or by any means without prior permission from the publisher.

Limit of Liability / Disclaimer of Warranty: While the publisher and the author have used their best efforts in preparing this book, they make no representations or warranties with respect to the accuracy or completeness of the contents of this book and specifically disclaim any implied warranties of merchantability or fitness for a particular purpose. The material contained herein may not be suitable for your situation. Neither the publisher nor the author shall be liable for any loss of profit or any other commercial damages, including but not limited to special, incidental, consequential, or other damages.

# Pongal: The Harvest Festival!

## Pongal is a harvest festival
## That celebrates the sun, the rain and the cattle!
## That reminds people to hail nature and be thankful,
## That makes every town festive and colorful!

**Pongal is celebrated between January 13 to 16
(these dates will vary in a leap year)**

Pongal: The Harvest Festival!

**This fun festival goes on for four days
When the Tamil people thank nature in many ways!
"Pongalo Pongal" is what everyone says
While seeking nature's blessings and grace!**

# Pongal: The Harvest Festival!

Clean homes, family gatherings and feasts
Celebrating the harvest and treats
With the festivities and fun, it greets
the warmer weather with celebration and sweets!

# Pongal: The Harvest Festival!

They thank the sun
They thank the rain
They thank the cattle
They gather the grain
'Cos its Pongal
Pongalo Pongal, Pongalo Pongal!

# Pongal: The Harvest Festival!

Pongal means abundance!

They clean their homes, and the surroundings
Bhogi is the first day of this four day festival
Out with the old and in with the new things,
To make room for the harvest that is plentiful!

**Bhogi Pongal: Clean and clutter free homes and new beginnings!**

Pongal: The Harvest Festival!

## They throw the old stuff in bonfire
## They are very careful not to cause a wildfire

## 'Cos its Bhogi Pongal
## Pongalo Pongal, Pongalo Pongal!

Pongal: The Harvest Festival!

They cook Sakkarai Pongal and offer to Sun
They thank nature for the good harvest
Surya Pongal is the second day of this festival
This is a day of feasts, fun and being thankful!

**Surya Pongal: Family gatherings, feasts, festivities and thankfulness!**

They eat the sugarcanes
and sweet Sakkarai Pongal
'Cos its Surya Pongal
Pongalo Pongal, Pongalo Pongal!

# Pongal: The Harvest Festival!

They dress up the cattle and pamper them all day
Maattu Pongal is celebrated on the third day!
Tractors have replaced the cattle today
But the tradition to thank cattle is here to stay

**Mattu Pongal: Celebrate, decorate and pamper cattle!**

They dress up the bulls, they dress up the cows
They take them around the town in their pretty bows

'Cos its Mattu Pongal
Pongalo Pongal, Pongalo Pongal!

Pongal: The Harvest Festival!

They meet the family, they meet the friends
They go around to many places until the day ends
Kaanum Pongal is the fourth day of this festival
It's the time for lots of fun, frolic and carnival!

**Kaanum Pongal: Family outings, Visiting friends and family!**

# Pongal: The Harvest Festival!

They make merry, they visit their siblings
They visit their elders and take their blessings

'Cos its Kaanum Pongal
Pongalo Pongal, Pongalo Pongal!

## Folklore on bulls and agriculture

*Shiva – a Hindu God, sent his bull – Basava, to the earth to tell the people of earth to massage their body with oil every day before bathing and eat food once in a month.*

*But Basava got it mixed up and told everyone that they should eat food everyday and have oil massage once in a month.*

*Shiva got upset with Basava for causing a need for more food on earth and sent him back to help the people of earth to cultivate more food so that they could eat every day!*

There are several lessons to be learned from the Pongal rituals and traditions.

The main lesson is to be thankful to nature. For without the sun, the rain and the cattle, life is impossible.

Bhogi tradition encourages us to keep our homes clutter free and clean. Painting the house regularly, kills mold and bacteria.

Cooking a big feast, meeting with family and friends promotes a society that nurtures relationships.

## Pongal Activities: Kolam - Free Hand Drawing

Kolam refers to intricate designs created using rice flour, white rock powder or colorful powders - typically drawn in front of the homes in India. In olden days, only rice flour was used to provide food for ants, insects and even little birds. These designs can range from being very simple to very complicated.

They are created as geometric shapes or free hand drawings using many different techniques. One can learn to create kolams with some practice. Here is a very simple design that can be practiced on paper and then tried with powder on any floor.

1. Draw two parallel lines of the same length.

　　　　　　_____
　　　　　　_____

2. Draw one shorter line on top in the middle of the longer lines and another shorter line at the bottom of the same length as the first short line.

　　　　　　_____
　　　　　　_____
　　　　　　_____
　　　　　　_____

# Pongal: The Harvest Festival!

3. Now, draw a slanting line connecting the beginning of the bottom short line to the end of the top long line and another slanting line connecting the beginning of the bottom long line and the end of the top short line as shown below.

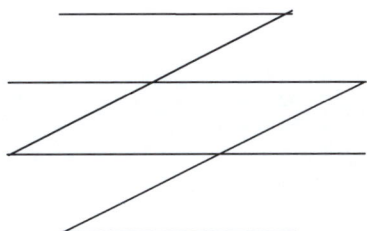

4. Draw two slanting lines connecting the short and long lines on the opposite side in a similar manner as shown below.

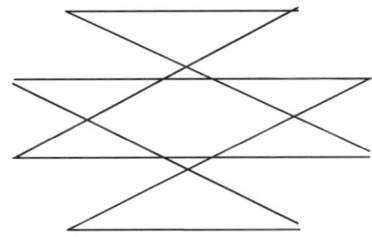

5. Make a tiny circle on the middle of the kolam and you are all done!

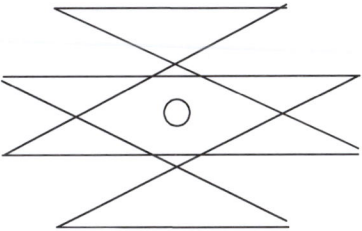

Pongal: The Harvest Festival!

## Pongal Activities: Draw a Pongal scene here.

# Pongal Activities: Write about the Pongal festival

# Pongal Activities: The Pongal Quiz

1. What is the name of the day of thanking the Sun?

2. Getting rid of the old things to make space for the new. Which day of Pongal celebrations does this statement apply to?

3. Pongal celebrations go on for:
    a. Two days
    b. Three days
    c. Four days

4. Maattu Pongal is celebrated to thank:
    a. Cats and dogs
    b. Bulls and Cows
    c. Elephants and Tigers

5. What do people eat on Surya Pongal day?
    a. Sakkarai Pongal and Sugarcane
    b. Sandwich and Salad
    c. Noodles and Cake

6. What lessons do Pongal celebrations teach us?

7. When is Pongal celebrated?
    a. December
    b. January
    c. May

Printed in Great Britain
by Amazon